Americans AT HOME

Four Hundred Years of American Houses

BY LEE PENNOCK HUNTINGTON

Coward, McCann & Geoghegan, Inc. · *New York*

For William
who combines the best
of old and new.

Photo Credits

Acorn Structures, Inc.: 33   California Redwood Society: 27   Jonathan Elliott: 34   Essex Institute: 10   Joe Ferlise: 31   Greenfield Village, Dearborn, Michigan: 12   Thomas Jefferson Memorial Foundation, Inc.: 11   James Kalett: 9   Library of Congress HABS Collection: 3, 4, 5, 8, 14, 17, 18, 21 (S. D. Butcher), 22, 23, 24, 29 (Blessing Studio)   Norman McGrath: 32   Merrimack Valley Textile Museum: 15   New Mexico Tourism & Travel Division, Commerce & Industry Department: 2   Newport Historical Society: 26   Paul Revere House: 4   Jacob A. Riis Collection, Museum of the City of New York: 20   St. Augustine Historical Society: 1   Julius Shulman: 30   Sleepy Hollow Restorations, Tarrytown, New York: 7   U. S. Department of Interior, National Park Service: 19   Vermont Division for Historic Preservation: 13 (Emma Jane Saxe), 16 (Courtney Fisher)   Jane Wattenberg: 25, 28

Library of Congress Cataloging in Publication Data
Huntington, Lee Pennock. Americans at home. Includes index. Summary: Explores the changing architectural styles found in American houses from colonial days to the present. 1. Architecture—United   States—Juvenile   literature.   [1.   Architecture.   2.   Dwellings]   I.   Title.
NA705.H87   728'.0973   81-4972   ISBN 0-698-20530-8   AACR2

Book design by Carolyn Craven   First Printing   Printed in the United States of America

CONTENTS

INTRODUCTION

What Kind of House?

THE KIND OF HOUSE YOU CHOOSE TO BUILD can reveal a lot about you and the world you live in. All across this land are millions of houses, old and new, that give a sense of our history and of the sort of people who have lived, worked, and made homes for themselves here.

In America, people wanted different kinds of houses at different times and places, and we have been free to experiment with a wonderful variety of buildings. No one could tell an American he or she ought to build just one "right" kind of house.

Over the years we have used some ideas from the Old World, some from the Indians of the New World, and we have invented others. Our range of climate, from cold and wet to hot and dry, means housing needs in one region may not be at all what they are in another. Construction has made use of an abundance of building materials—stone, adobe, brick, and many kinds of wood.

But a house is more than a shelter. It is also a symbol of how the people who built it and live in it react to the world around them and how they think of themselves. We have had changing ideas of ourselves and of what is beautiful or useful, and this has found expression in our houses. Americans first lived in simple houses made of local materials. Then, as the country became more prosperous, those who could afford to do so built houses that provided much more than a roof overhead. A choice of architectural style could reveal the owner's taste, education, or business success. In the nineteenth century houses became more and more elaborate; some were even castles. Now as we near the end of the twentieth century with more people and less space, we can see that we are using up natural resources and need to conserve energy. We are once again building simpler houses.

In every period the great majority of houses, built by ordinary people, were small and unpretentious. But the fine houses built by wealthy property owners set the style in their day. Sooner or later other houses were built in smaller and less expensive versions of the great houses, until after a time a new style would become fashionable. It is often these fine houses that have survived and that we can see today.

No one style, then, can be called "American architecture." Instead, we have a heritage of fascinating diversity, from log cabins to Victorian mansions to the solar-heated homes of today. It would take years to study them in detail, but looking at a few representative houses can help us begin to be aware of what building a home has meant and still means to Americans.

1 · EARLY COLONIAL HOMES
1600–1720

St. Augustine

WE OFTEN THINK OF THE PILGRIMS AS THE first colonists in America, but the oldest existing city in the country is St. Augustine, in Florida. Spaniards came here in 1565 and cleared small fields in the tropical wilderness. The soldiers and their families first lived in crude thatched wooden huts put up around a fort. Later, a natural shellstone, called coquina, was discovered on a nearby island and settlers began using it to build their houses.

The oldest house still standing today in St. Augustine was built of coquina by Tomas Gonzales y Hernandez on the site of an earlier palm-thatched hut. He wanted it to be as much as possible like the houses he had known in Spain. He made the coquina walls thick and solid, knowing this would help to keep the house cool in the hot Florida climate. The floors were of tabia, a mixture of sand, shell, and lime, as they often were in Spain. The cedar woodwork was also like that of Spanish houses. There was no fireplace, for the Spaniards used charcoal braziers for cooking.

7

The kitchen opened out onto a walled patio, where orange, lemon, pomegranate, and fig trees grew along with herbs and flowers. At the windows were heavy wooden shutters to keep out storms and enemies.

Over the next three hundred years, many changes were made in the house, including the addition of a second story and a shingled roof. But if you visit it today, you will still see a house of traditional Spanish character which served well for generations of Spaniards in the New World. *(1)*

1   Oldest Spanish house in the United States, St. Augustine, Florida

Santa Fe

THE SECOND OLDEST CITY IN THE UNITED
States is Santa Fe, in dry and sunny New Mexico. It too was
settled by Spaniards, although native Americans were there long
before, living in pueblos, villages built along canyon walls or in
valleys. A pueblo consisted of a series of connected units with
walls made of sun-dried clay. Beams of cedar logs, called vigas,
extended out beyond the walls. These beams were covered with
layers of branches, grass, and a top coating of mud plaster to
make a flat roof. The Pueblo Indians had developed an ideal
construction for their climate, for the thick walls absorbed midday
heat and at night slowly released it into the rooms while outside
the temperature might drop as much as forty degrees.

When Don Pedro de Peralta, Spanish governor of the province
of New Mexico, began in 1609 to build the capital city of Santa
Fe, he used both Indian and Spanish designs and techniques. The
Pueblo workmen learned the Spanish method of using wooden
forms to make bricks of clay, sand, and straw, which were then
dried in the sun. These were called adobe bricks.

The walled town was constructed like Spanish towns around a
large open space called a plaza. There were quarters for soldiers,
storehouses, a chapel, and a building called a palacio where the
governor lived and had his offices. In the beginning the palacio
had a great heavy gate but no windows, for the building also
served as a fortress. During an Indian uprising of 1680, nearly
a thousand Spanish colonists took refuge there. But as times became more peaceful, the walls were opened up with windows.

The governor's residence was one story high and about 800 feet
long. Like the Indian buildings, the roof was flat, with beams
extending outward. There was an enclosed patio in the rear, and

2 *Governor's Palace, Santa Fe, New Mexico*

a later addition was a long Spanish-style gallery, or covered porch, along the plaza side, where people gathered in the shade.

For 130 years this huge adobe building was used as a residence for Spanish governors. Later, other officials lived there, and today it is a museum. It is a massive, proud building, expressing both the closeness to the earth of the Pueblo Indians and the power of the Spanish rulers. *(2)*

Virginia

ENGLISH SETTLERS CAME TO VIRGINIA IN 1607. There they found a temperate climate, rivers full of fish, and forests full of great trees. At first they made themselves lean-tos of poles covered with branches and dirt. Then they made crude small houses with walls and roofs of wattle and daub. Wattle and daub was a weaving of twigs and sticks plastered with clay, and was a building method that had been commonly used in England for centuries.

It was not long before the settlers improved their shelters by building houses with strong wooden frames like the ones they had known in England. In 1615, one of the Virginians wrote that the settlement of Jamestown "hath in it two fair rows of houses, all of framed timber, two stories, an upper garret or corn-loft high."

Stones were scarce, so clay was dug from the riverbanks to make bricks. One of the very first brick houses was built by young Adam Thoroughgood, who had come over from England as an indentured servant. After working long enough to gain his freedom, he became one of the leaders of the community.

In 1636, remembering the handsome brick houses of England, Adam built a two-story house with two rooms on each floor. But there were differences in Adam's New World house. Because the Indians of Virginia were not friendly to the settlers, Adam had loopholes for firing guns in the walls of the upper rooms, and hiding places were built between the walls next to the fireplaces.

This house, with its huge end chimneys, three-foot-thick walls, casement windows with wooden shutters, and fine brickwork, still stands today in Princess Anne County, proof that a young man who arrived with nothing could make his fortune in Virginia. *(3)*

Some Virginians had to be content with small wooden houses and a few acres of farmland. Others cleared land along the riverbanks and raised tobacco to send to England. The more successful planters increased their land holdings and built larger houses, but it was not until the next century that the great plantation houses were built in Virginia and elsewhere in the South.

New England and Long Island

THOSE WHO CAME FROM ENGLAND TO MAS-
sachusetts Bay left behind a mild climate, open fields, and long-

settled communities. Here they found rocky shores, an endless stretch of forest, and snow that lay upon the land for months on end. Their immediate need was for shelter quickly put together. With such abundance of wood, you might think they would build log cabins. But these Englishmen had never seen log cabins, so to begin with they lived in dugouts or in crude huts of sticks and reeds, like the dwellings of the Indians who lived along the coves where they fished and raised corn.

3   Adam Thoroughgood House, Princess Anne County, Virginia

As soon as they could spare time from clearing land and planting crops, the settlers built sturdier houses of the kind they were used to in England. English country houses, which had been built almost the same way since the Middle Ages, had massive oak frames and huge central chimneys. The windows were casements, opening out, with small diamond-shaped panes of glass. Walls were made of wattle and daub or of sun-baked brick. Roofs were covered with heavy layers of grass thatch.

But however fondly they remembered their English homes, the newcomers found they had to make some changes in the traditional designs. The great problem in New England was to keep warm during the winter. There was plenty of wood to build the frame of a house, but the northern winds found chinks in the wattle and daub walls. Soon the builders discovered a more solid barrier against the weather. They cut boards and fastened them with wooden pegs or hand-forged nails, each board overlapping the one below, to cover all the outside walls. This kind of exterior board is known as clapboard, and it was not long before it was used everywhere in New England.

Windows were small, with oiled paper brought from England instead of glass, and heavy wooden shutters that could be closed in harsh weather or in case of an impending Indian attack. The settlers found that the hot summer sun dried out thatched roofs, making it easy for chimney sparks to start a fire, so they began covering their roofs with wooden shingles.

Many settlers started with one-room houses and later enlarged them. Rooms might be added to the sides or back of the original room, or a whole second floor might be built. A big chimney was often built in the center of the house, with fireplaces opening off into several rooms. In a two-story house, the stairway was a set of very small wedge-shaped steps leading to the rooms

4   *Paul Revere House, Boston, Massachusetts*

above, which served as bedrooms and storage rooms for provisions.

Large families lived close together in these low-ceilinged rooms. The main room, called a keeping room, was used for countless activities—cooking, eating, spinning, weaving, candlemaking, dyeing, soapmaking. Some members of the family slept there too, and sometimes on frosty nights small farm animals were brought in to sleep with them. There were no closets, and no such thing as a bathroom or indoor toilet.

These early houses with their steep roofs and few tiny windows look severe and closed-in to us today. The people who lived in them were not yet at home in this dangerous new country. Inside their strong walls and the rooms with heavy wooden beams, they carried on their daily work and family life much as they had in old England.

One such house was built in 1676 in Boston. It was later bought by Paul Revere, and visitors can still see the steep roof, small-paned windows, and cramped dark rooms. *(4)*

14

As the years went by, the New England colonists became more independent from the mother country. They gained confidence as they found they could provide for their families from fields that gave them good harvests, and from rivers and forests where there was plenty of fish and game. They became experienced in managing their own affairs of government, church, and business, even though they were subject to the king far away in England.

English settlers spread out from Massachusetts Bay to Connecticut, Long Island, Rhode Island, Maine, and New Hampshire. Often they went in groups to establish a new church congregation in what was usually wilderness. Land was cleared and villages laid out according to plan, with a central open green space called a common. Here the meetinghouse was built, with houses set around the common in neat formation. Each house had its garden for vegetables, herbs, and flowers, and each family farmed its own fields, which lay at the outskirts of the village. These were self-sufficient communities where people shared their lives and carried on a democratic tradition.

Sometimes people built their own houses, but most were made by the village carpenter. The old sharp gables and heavy-looking roofs were disappearing. Now people lived in new houses which looked less like the old English types. Casement windows were replaced by sash windows that opened up and down, with panes of glass fixed in wooden frames.

Perhaps the most enduring style developed in the New England area was that of the Cape Cod house. Many of these small square houses, with roofs that came right down to the front door and windows, were constructed on Cape Cod, south of Boston. English cottages of this shape had been built of stone, but here they were made of wood, or sometimes of brick. The rooms were built around a central chimney. There was little headroom under the sloping eaves, so dormer windows were often built in the roof to give the bedrooms a little more space and light. This compact little house, not difficult to build, was snug and warm when winter winds blew. It could be enlarged outward with wings at either side, or by an ell at the back. Often these basic houses had numerous additional rooms added to shelter growing families, while retaining the original center square as the heart of the house. *(5)*

One of the ways to enlarge a two-story house was to add a lean-to at the back. The roof was then continued down and the space beneath enclosed. This gave the house an outline which reminded people of the containers in which they kept their salt,

5   Fitch House, Cohasset, Massachusetts

so a house of this sort came to be called a saltbox house.

In the village of East Hampton on Long Island, New York, a saltbox house was built about 1655. Its great central chimney had fireplaces opening into five rooms. Many years later, the house was owned by the family of John Howard Payne, who grew up to write "Home, Sweet Home." It was this modest gray-shingled saltbox house he was remembering when he wrote the song that still touches American hearts everywhere (6)

These village houses were all functional, that is, they were designed for practical use, with no unnecessary spaces or ornamentation. Their beauty lay in their well-balanced proportions and simplicity. They speak of the hardworking character of the people who lived in them, their honesty, and lack of pretense.

6 *Saltbox house, John Howard Payne's "Home Sweet Home," East Hampton, New York*

Middle Atlantic

THE EARLIEST HOUSES OF THE DELAWARE
River region were log cabins. In 1638 the first settlers came there
from Scandinavia, where the great northern forests had provided
plenty of wood for housebuilding. The Scandinavians had long
ago developed ways to build simple houses of logs.

After the logs were cut and trimmed with an ax, they were
notched at the ends and then fitted together to make walls. Spaces
between the logs were chinked with bits of wood and moss, then
plastered with mud or clay. Roofs were usually quite steeply
pitched so that rain or snow would run off, and they were shingled
with bark. Sometimes the only opening was a door. If there were
windows, they were small and covered with oiled deerhide. A
large chimney of either log or stone was built at one end of the
cabin. The big stone fireplace was the center of cooking and family
life. The floor was generally of hard-packed dirt, and a ladder
led to a sleeping loft.

Almost anyone could make a log cabin, so later arrivals from
other countries copied the Scandinavian methods. Log cabins were
built in stump-filled clearings throughout the wilderness areas of
America. The log cabin became the symbol of the hardy pioneers
who could make shelters for their families using the materials they
found in the forest.

New York

IN THE COLONY OF NEW YORK, SETTLERS
from Holland in 1625 began building the town of New Amster-
dam where New York City stands today. They became prosper-

ous traders and built houses in rows like the ones in Holland, two stories high, of stone, wood, and later brick, with stepped gables and many chimneys.

A number of the Dutch families moved out to land along the Hudson River, where they established farms. Stephanus Van Cortlandt, the first American-born mayor of New York City, for years bought acreage along the river or traded with the Indians for it in exchange for guns, rum, clothing, and wampum. Eventually he amassed more than 87,000 acres. In 1697 King William III of England rewarded Stephanus for his services to the Crown by giving him the title of Lord of the Manor of Cortlandt. This meant that Stephanus had control over all the fish, game, and timber within this vast property.

Land was cleared and rented to tenant farmers. Sawmills and flour mills were built, a dairy, brick kiln, and blacksmith shop constructed. Boats took lumber, grain, and flour up and down the river to New York City and Albany. A whole community of several hundred people lived and worked on the Van Cortlandt estate.

The center of activity was the Van Cortlandt manor house. This originally had been a simple stone building which was used as a trading station for the furs brought there by Indians. A second story was added later, with roof beams hewn from timber cut in the family forests. Although Stephanus Van Cortlandt's descendants enlarged the house, plastered the interior walls, and added second-story porches reached by twin sets of steps, they never made it into a grand mansion.

In the old downstairs part of the house, visitors can still see the kitchen with its enormous fireplace, a milk room with cobbled floor, and a family room. Upstairs are the parlor, dining room, and bedrooms. Out in back are a smokehouse and what was called a "necessary house," or privy. For many generations the Van Cortlandts lived in this farmhouse, a simple but handsome country home fit for the industrious Dutch family which supervised all that went on in their little kingdom. *(7)*

7 Van Cortlandt Manor, Tarrytown, New York

2 · THE EIGHTEENTH CENTURY

IN THE EIGHTEENTH CENTURY, MANY changes took place as the population of the country grew and people could begin to think about being comfortable rather than just surviving. Some of them were doing well enough to want to be more than comfortable. They wished to be fashionable too. Ships bringing from England such luxuries as silken gowns and waistcoats, wigs, silver, and china also brought books filled with pictures of the latest architectural styles in what was known as the Palladian manner.

Andrea Palladio was an Italian architect who lived during the sixteenth century, in that great period of renewed activity in the arts known as the Renaissance. Palladio's work was based on the strict forms of ancient Roman temples and public buildings. Beginning in the reign of King James I, seventeenth-century English architects took Palladio's designs and adapted them for both city and country dwellings.

Palladian houses were symmetrical, the number of windows balancing each other on both sides of a central doorway. The entrance was made important by a portico, or roof, often supported by columns, crowned by a triangular pediment or scroll. Windows were framed with moldings. One kind of Palladian window was a large triple window, the middle one generally arched. A Palladian building did not have a steep pitched roof and gables. Instead there was what was called a hip roof, sloping upward from all four sides of the building.

The typical Palladian house had a large entrance hallway from which rose a fine stairway with carved balusters and newel posts. Beams were covered with plaster ceilings, and rooms were paneled with wood. Moldings were placed around doors, windows, and cupboards, and fireplaces were framed in wood. The effect was much lighter, more spacious, and elegant than the houses of the early colonists.

When the Americans eagerly studied the English architecture books, they found the Palladian designs very pleasing. It was not long before they were asking their carpenters to copy them in houses with larger rooms, higher ceilings, more chimneys, bigger windows with larger panes, and far more decoration inside and out than their grandfathers had known. There were increasing numbers of capable designers, builders, and skillful craftsmen in the thirteen colonies, and they produced many handsome buildings in a style which became known as Georgian because it was popular during the reigns of three English kings, George I, George II, and George III.

Houses of this style in England were generally made of stone or even marble. In America, they were often built of brick, but if the owner could not afford that, exteriors were made of wood, sometimes cut, carved, and painted to look like stone. If the exterior was finished with wooden clapboards, they might be painted in pleasant tones of gray, blue, green, salmon, or yellow, with white trim. In rural areas, especially in Pennsylvania and along the Hudson River, fieldstone was used to build simplified Georgian houses. There was considerable regional variety as Americans adapted the Georgian designs to their own needs and abilities.

In Virginia, Maryland, and North and South Carolina, during the Georgian period, large-scale plantations were established by farmers who had become prosperous raising tobacco, rice, or indigo through the labor of their slaves, brought over from Africa. Such a plantation owner wanted to have as large and impressive a house as possible, from which he could manage his vast property and entertain a stream of relatives and other visitors. A plantation might be miles from the nearest neighbor or town, so it contained numerous buildings and workshops to house the necessary activities of a self-contained community. Kilns were set up for the baking of bricks made from local clay by the slaves. Millions of these bricks went into the handsome Georgian houses of the South. The slaves themselves were generally housed in very humble, often miserable, cabins with no conveniences, at what the plantation owners considered a suitable distance from the main house.

Throughout the South, especially in the city of Charleston, South Carolina, and in the Northeast there are still many examples of fine Georgian houses to be seen. Some are modestly elegant, others more ambitious. One of the most splendid is Mount Pleasant, the Philadelphia house built in 1761 by a flamboyant one-armed seaman named John MacPherson, who had made his fortune as a privateer. Mount Pleasant, with its imposing proportions and yellow stucco walls set off with blocks of red brick, is notable for its handsome pediment and Palladian window. The gifted Philadelphia artisans made certain that every detail was perfect

23

8   Mount Pleasant, Philadelphia, Pennsylvania

inside and out. Unfortunately, MacPherson spent so lavishly on his house—£14,000, an enormous sum for those days—that he had to sell it when it was finished. But like other, less grandiose Georgian houses, it proclaimed that Americans knew what was good architectural style and that they could build houses just as beautiful as those across the ocean. *(8)*

Still, there were great numbers of Americans who did not try to imitate London taste by building Georgian houses. In New York and New Jersey, farmhouses were frequently in the Dutch style, built of whitewashed stone with long low roofs. Both English

9 *Farmhouse and connected farm buildings, Bridgton, Maine*

and German settlers in Pennsylvania built sturdy stone houses overshadowed by immense barns. Farmhouses in New England, nearly always of wood, often were connected to the barn and sheds to make it easier to care for animals and to visit the woodpile during the winter. This system later became known as "continuous architecture." *(9)*

The country was still young, not yet independent. There were many more farmers and villagers than city dwellers. When they built, most people thought in practical terms and not about architectural style.

25

3 · FEDERAL HOUSES

1790–1820

DURING THE YEARS OF THE REVOLUTION-
ary war, nobody had much time to build. When the war was
over, Americans were free of English rulers, taxes, and armies.
But they did not immediately try out new American ways of doing
everything. They still looked to England for ideas regarding dress,
literature, art, and architecture. The Georgian style of architecture
remained popular, but new influences also came on the scene.

Two Scottish brothers, Robert and James Adam, had studied
the remains of late Roman houses excavated in Pompeii and other
cities and found that these houses were far more elaborately designed and decorated than had been realized. In the 1760s and
70s the Adam brothers applied these design ideas to the creation
of beautiful English houses. They refined the solid Georgian style,
making rooms in round or oval shapes and using much carved or
raised plaster ornamentation. The Adam style also incorporated
French and Italian Renaissance ideas: An Adam house was full
of decorative patterns of garlands, sheaves of wheat, festoons,
rosettes, and urns.

In the United States, the Adam style was called Federal in honor of the new republic of federated states. It was highly popular during the early decades of our nation. Americans who did well in business often decided to announce their success by building handsome Federal houses, usually on the best streets in town.

Today the streets of Salem, Massachusetts, are still lined with Federal houses of great elegance. From this seaport town, merchants sent out fleets of clipper ships to trade with far countries. One of these merchants was Jerathmeel Peirce, whose fortune was made in the East India trade.

Peirce wanted a home as solid and splendid as his business success, and in Salem there lived a young builder who could construct a house to satisfy him. Samuel McIntire was a wood-carver, a craftsman of great skill, who studied books on architecture and became a superb builder.

McIntire designed a large, impressive house for Mr. Peirce. It was three stories high, with fourteen windows across the front, and tall chimneys. At each corner of the house was a massive Greek pilaster. All across the top was a balustrade enclosing a roof deck where Mr. Peirce could stand and peer through his telescope at his clipper ships sailing across Massachusetts Bay. The beautifully proportioned rooms had fireplaces carved by Samuel McIntire himself. McIntire also made all the doorways and cornices, and even the wooden urns on the fence posts. He went on to design and build many other houses for prosperous families, making Salem one of the most attractive towns in the new nation. *(10)*

During this period, a number of architects came from abroad to live and work in the United States. Irishman James Hoban designed the White House, Englishman Benjamin Latrobe was the chief architect of the Capitol, and a Frenchman, Pierre Charles L'Enfant, laid out the plan of Washington, D.C. Earlier, most

American architects had been amateurs with a talent for design. There was still no American architectural school and would not be until 1866. But now a group of full-time professionals with sound European training in technical and engineering skills entered the field; these architects were recognized as specialists who expected to be paid professional fees for their work.

Still, there were native-born Americans whose architectural work was influential in the new republic. Boston's Charles Bulfinch, whose European travels inspired some of his finest work, completed Latrobe's Capitol project in Washington. He also designed the Massachusetts State House with its golden dome, and many houses for wealthy Bostonians. Bulfinch's imaginative layouts for these houses included soaring spiral staircases and rooms that were round, oval, or even octagonal.

Another American architect, Asher Benjamin, built fine

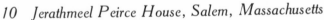

10 Jerathmeel Peirce House, Salem, Massachusetts

churches and houses. In 1797 Benjamin wrote *The Country Builder's Assistant*, a handbook of instructions for carpenters. This guide was immensely popular, and all over New England buildings sprang up in the fashionable Federal style based on Benjamin's drawings. If an owner could afford it, his house was of brick. Otherwise, it was of wood, painted yellow, slate blue, or deep red, with gleaming white trim.

The most renowned amateur architect was the author of the Declaration of Independence and third president of the United States, Thomas Jefferson. "Architecture is my delight," declared Jefferson, and in a lifetime of its practice he revealed great vision and skill. As a young Virginia gentleman in 1769, he began building his own house on his father's estate. He called it Monticello—"little hill." Jefferson trained his slaves as bricklayers, stonecutters, masons, cabinetmakers, and ironworkers. He worked on Monticello for nearly forty years, remodeling and adding on but retaining the basic Palladian plan.

Living for five years in France as the diplomatic representative of the new United States, Jefferson was impressed by French adaptations of classical Greek and Roman art and architecture. While traveling widely in Europe, he much admired the Roman ruins he studied there and became "a true lover of antiquity." He thought the noble Roman buildings were a fitting expression of the simplicity and strength of the Roman government. Jefferson felt that the architecture of the new republic of the United States should reflect the same ideals as those of the old republic of Rome. So he had little to do with the sophisticated Federal style. He built Monticello with a domed roof and a portico with strong white columns in the old Roman style. Americans, studying pictures of Monticello, took a great interest in the home of their former president and considered it the most beautiful house in America. *(11)*

Jefferson designed many other buildings, including the superb campus of the University of Virginia. A practical and remarkably inventive man, he designed buildings that were not merely handsome but also comfortable and efficient.

Jefferson's patriotic vision of how the new republic should be represented in its architecture had a great influence upon other designers. A whole group of younger architects began to turn away from the English fashions and think instead in terms of what best would represent a democratic society.

Not everyone was concerned with such matters. As towns grew crowded and arable farmland diminished, Americans began mov-

11 (below) Thomas Jefferson's Monticello, Charlottesville, Virginia
12 (right) William Holmes McGuffey log cabin birthplace, West Alexandrea, Pennsylvania

ing westward. The great unbroken forests fell before the pioneers' axes. Farms and villages were built along the frontier in Ohio, western Pennsylvania, West Virginia, Kentucky, Michigan, Indiana, and as far west as St. Louis. One-room log cabins housed large families which were too busy and too short of money to give a thought to architectural style. In one such Pennsylvania cabin William Holmes McGuffey was born in 1800. He grew up to become a great educator, his *Readers* known to pupils in schoolrooms throughout the country. *(12)*

In politics, a log cabin birth proved to be an asset for several of our presidents, including, of course, Abraham Lincoln.

For many years in the nineteenth century, a log cabin was still the easiest and cheapest sort of shelter to build, and if a family found the land they had claimed was not satisfactory, they didn't have to leave behind many material possessions when they pulled up roots and tried settling somewhere else. Some wanted to be entirely free of society: Abraham Lincoln's father said, "If you can see the smoke of another man's cabin, it's time to move on." And move on he did. Other Americans did the same, pushing the frontier even farther west.

4 · THE GREEK REVIVAL

1820–1860

WITH THE NINETEENTH CENTURY, THE AGE of the machine arrived. Factories and mills sprang up along every stream and river where water power could be harnessed. The factory techniques developed in England's recent Industrial Revolution were adopted and improved upon in the United States as clever Yankees invented new and better machines and steam engines. Many things that had always been made at home or by artisans—cloth, building materials, furniture—could now be mass-produced by machines and sold at low prices.

Canals and railroads opened up ever larger areas of the country. In the North, Americans were manufacturing and trading at an exhilarating pace. There were jobs for anyone willing to work, and people who took them made more money than they would by staying on farms. Immigrants came by the thousands, drawn by stories of great opportunities in the new nation. The democracy forged by the Revolution was working more successfully than its detractors had foreseen. Other countries were looking at the United States with respect, and Americans felt an intense pride in their independence and prosperity.

In every school and college, students learned about the very first democracy the world had ever known—that of ancient Greece. Americans felt a kinship with the Greek citizens who had decided to do away with kings and run their own affairs. They felt their elected officials in Washington were carrying on the great traditions of the leaders of ancient Athens.

Teachers, artists, and writers spread the results of studies and excavations in Greece, bringing to light more and more of that long-ago culture. Benjamin Latrobe, a leader of the small group of professional architects now at work in the United States, envisioned a time when "Greece may be revived in the woods of America." He and his pupil William Strickland turned more and more to Greek design for inspiration.

Strickland's design for a bank in Philadelphia was a copy of a famous Greek building, the Parthenon, which had two facades, each lined by a row of eight splendid columns. The president of the bank, Nicholas Biddle, was so pleased that he declared, "The two great truths of the world are the Bible and Grecian architecture." Mr. Biddle had his own family house completely made over with Greek columns so that it too looked like a Greek temple—or a bank.

Asher Benjamin produced a series of new books, *The Practice of Architecture* (1830), *The Practical House Carpenter* (1830), *The Builder's Guide* (1839) and *Elements of Architecture* (1843), in which the Grecian style was explained in practical terms. Minard Lafever, a self-taught designer and builder from New York State, who had already written two highly popular building guides, published *The Beauties of Modern Architecture* in 1835. By mod-

ern architecture, Lafever meant the Grecian style, and he provided accurate and detailed instructions for building such houses from sawn lumber. These books had a wide influence. Pictures of buildings in the Greek style were carefully studied not only by architects and designers but by all sorts of ordinary Americans. "This is how I want my house to look," a new homeowner would say to a carpenter, pointing to a sketch in a book by Benjamin or Lafever. And the carpenter would do his best, which was often very good, to reproduce the design not in the marble of the Greeks but in American wood painted white. *(13)*

This movement, which became known as the Greek Revival, began in the Northeast and spread quickly throughout the rest of the country. It did not matter that the outlines of a Greek temple might not seem appropriate in a snowy New England village or on the muddy street of a new town in the Midwest. Or that the big square rooms were hard to heat and the heavy portico with its

34

13　*Greek Revival house,
Castleton, Vermont*

rows of columns shut out the sunlight from the front of the house.
The manufacturer, banker, lawyer, professor, or farmer who could
afford it desired a house that would reflect "the glory that was
Greece," and also his own.

Waves of settlers from the East built new communities beyond
the Appalachian Mountains. Whole towns were built in the Greek
Revival style along the Ohio River and in every part of the Midwest. State capitols, courthouses, college buildings, banks, and
private houses all tried to express the noble simplicity of the Greek
ideal.

But already there were signs of the differences that separated
the states and that would one day explode into the Civil War.
The invention of the mechanical cotton gin made it possible for one
worker to clean five hundred pounds of cotton daily instead of the
five pounds per day he could do by hand. This meant that scores
of big factories making cotton textiles opened in the North. And

it meant that in the South, planters expanded their cotton fields enormously and bought more and more slaves to help grow and pick the cotton. The nation was soon divided into slave states and free states.

Andrew Jackson, born in a log cabin, became a military hero, the first representative to Congress from Tennessee, and the seventh president of the United States. His home near Nashville was a plantation called The Hermitage, where he grew cotton. The first two houses Jackson built were destroyed by fire, and in 1835 he built another in Greek Revival style. His house has a two-story portico at both front and rear, each with six shapely pillars. The rooms are spacious and high-ceilinged. A fine spiral staircase

14   The Hermitage, Andrew Jackson's home, Nashville, Tennessee

curves up from the wide hallway, which is papered with scenes from a Greek legend. A green lawn surrounds the house, and the garden is laid out in an acre of flowers. In Jackson's time, the slaves who tended the house and grounds and worked in the cotton fields lived in log cabins. One of the cabins, still standing today not far from the main house, belonged to "Uncle Alfred," Jackson's favorite slave, who lived to be nearly one hundred. *(14)*

The Hermitage was only one of the many Greek Revival mansions which arose in the South from Maryland to New Orleans. Most of the newly rich planters who built these magnificent homes did so because they were beautiful and fashionable, not necessarily because they admired Greek democratic ideals.

In the North, most Americans still lived on farms or in small villages, but the cities were growing rapidly. Shiploads of immigrants from England, Ireland, and elsewhere in Europe arrived to build railroads, dig in coal mines, and work in factories. Workers were crowded into old houses or in cheaply built new ones. Entire families might live in one dark room without heat or water. The owners of such buildings did little to care for them, and whole sections of cities such as New York became slums.

But in several New England communities the factory owners tried to provide good housing for their workers. In the town of Lowell, Massachusetts, it was mostly young unmarried farm girls who first came to work in the new textile factories. The mill owners provided well-built brick boardinghouses where these girls could live simply but quite comfortably. The mill owners, who thought of themselves as fathers of big families of workers, also had built near their factories rows of brick houses which married workers could rent or buy. This sort of arrangement became known as a "company town," because the company had so much to say about

15   Merrimack mills and boarding houses, Lowell, Massachusetts

how its workers lived. But even though the factory hands labored for twelve or fourteen hours a day, and their wages were low, they were better off by far than the slaves in the South. *(15)*

5 · THE ROMANTIC ERA

1820–1860

AT THE SAME TIME THE GREEK REVIVAL WAS strongly influencing architecture throughout the land, some Americans became interested in quite a different style. The years between 1820 and 1860 became known as the Romantic era because people took a romantic interest in the history and fashions of the Middle Ages. Americans enthusiastically read books about medieval kings and queens, knights and ladies. Those who went abroad to take the Grand Tour of all the famous cities of Europe came back to tell of the glorious medieval buildings they had seen, built in the Gothic style.

Gothic cathedrals and castles were marvels of engineering, built of carefully cut blocks of stone, with tall towers and spires. Exterior walls were richly decorated with stone carvings and moldings. Windows were in the form of pointed arches. Interiors had high vaulted ceilings supported by massive stone columns. These buildings, which might take fifty or more years to build, were strong, magnificent, dignified, and enduring.

Newly rich Americans recalled the old English saying that "a man's home is his castle." What better way to spend money than to build a home that really looked like a Gothic castle? For these Americans the stark simplicity of Greek Revival architecture would not do.

In the 1840s and 50s, Alexander Jackson Davis, one of the most popular architects of the new Gothic Revival style, built castles for a carpet manufacturer in New York City, a leather dealer in Connecticut, a planter in Virginia, a mill owner in Massachusetts, and a wholesale druggist in New Jersey. And when these millionaires gave money to build a church, they asked him to build that too in Gothic Revival style.

People who weren't millionaires also admired this style. Their "castles" had to be considerably smaller and constructed of wood. Fortunately, they could consult a builder's handbook. *Cottage Residences*, written in 1842 by landscape gardener Andrew Jackson Downing and illustrated by his friend Davis, provided pictures and instructions for building modest houses in this manner. The builders of wooden Gothic Revival houses used their imaginations in adding the trim that imitated medieval stone traceries. Eaves and gables were adorned with fanciful edgings that were cut from wood with a scroll saw. People who thought this a poor imitation of the real thing called it "gingerbread," and laughed at these examples of "Carpenter Gothic" or "wedding cake" houses. But the owners were pleased with their fashionable architecture, and felt more stylish than those who were still living in Georgian, Federal, or Greek Revival houses. *(16)*

It was about this time that a new kind of construction was developed. Until the nineteenth century, the basis of any building had been the strong wooden frame. Huge logs had to be cut and sawed by hand. Then these heavy beams were lifted into place

16 Gothic Revival house, Windsor, Vermont

and fitted together with wooden pegs and hand-forged nails. It took the labor of many men to prepare the materials and to put together a sizable house. Now there were machines that could saw lumber into uniform lengths, other machines that could turn out nails by the thousands. In 1839 a Chicago builder used these materials in a new method called balloon framing. A balloon frame was constructed of far lighter weight wood than was used in the past. It was said that "a man and a boy can now attain the same results, with ease, that twenty men could on an old-fashioned frame."

At first people were uneasy about this framing, fearing it was not strong enough to last. But as it proved nearly as sturdy and was so much easier and quicker to construct, the balloon frame was soon accepted by everyone and the heavy hand-hewn frame became a thing of the past.

41

In 1848 another new building technique was used for the first time. This was the cast-iron frame that could support much heavier weights than wood, and it made possible buildings of several stories. One day steel frames would be used in skyscrapers.

Another style that was welcomed before the Civil War was the Italianate, inspired by the Renaissance country houses of northern Italy. The American version was quite a large house, perhaps of brick. There was usually an off-center square tower and a nearly flat roof with heavy overhanging eaves supported by brackets. The tall windows were often round-arched, and there might be bay windows as well. Sometimes there were balconies or a cupola, and nearly always a veranda or porch.

Large houses in the Italianate style, set back from the street in spacious lawns, were built for over thirty years in many towns and cities by people who thought of themselves as knowing something about art and architecture. An Italianate house had space for entertaining guests in the formal parlor and dining room, enough bedrooms to accommodate a numerous family, and quarters in back for the hired girl. This style, built during the years when Queen Victoria reigned in England, is what people often think of now as a "Victorian" house. *(17)*

17   Italianate house, Portland, Maine

6 · THE AGE OF EXPANSION

1865–1900

THE CIVIL WAR MARKED THE END OF SLAV-ery and an end to a way of living in the South. It was no longer possible for a plantation owner to keep slaves to work in his fields or take care of his big house. Many of the plantation houses were abandoned. Nearly everyone in the South was poor now, and few new houses were built.

In the North, the years after the war were a time of greater prosperity than ever. New businesses were started, old ones were expanded. There was great confidence in the future of the country. Resources such as lumber, coal, and water seemed to have no limit. The West was opening up, and there was land enough for everyone. Immigrants were coming to our shores by the thousands, so labor was cheap. If there were any problems, scientists and engineers would surely solve them. America was the fastest-growing nation in the world and certain to be one of the richest.

It was a time when men wore carefully tended beards and

always appeared in public in formal clothes. Women squeezed themselves into corsets and dressed in elaborate gowns crowned with flowered and feathered bonnets. Children wore stiff suits or dresses covered with embroidery, lace, puffs, and ribbons. Sofas were upholstered in silk or damask, chairs and tables were heavily carved. Houses built at this time were frequently just as ornate as the clothing and furniture.

An architectural style much favored in this period was the Second Empire, copied from buildings constructed in Paris during the reign of Emperor Napoleon III (1852–70). One of the most noticeable things about this style was the use of a high roof, which sat like a four-sided hat atop the building. This was called a mansard roof, after the French architect Francois Mansart. The top floor under this roof was usually used for bedrooms, and had dormer windows. Houses built in this style had many high windows, often crowned with impressive moldings. Americans liked porches, so they frequently added these to their houses, although such a thing would never be seen in Paris. *(18)*

In the second half of the nineteenth century, rows of brownstone houses were erected on city streets, particularly in the New York area. They were built of brown or reddish sandstone, usually four stories high and perhaps with a mansard roof. These houses were narrow, not wider than two rooms with a hallway. Kitchen and dining room were on the first floor, drawing room on the second, family rooms on the third, children's nursery and servants' quarters on the top floor. There was a small yard or garden behind each house, separated from its neighbors by fences.

It was in such a brownstone house in New York City that our twenty-sixth president, Theodore Roosevelt, was born in 1858. All his life he remembered his boyhood home—especially the high-ceilinged drawing room, with its sparkling mirrors and crystal

18   *Second Empire mansard house, St. Louis, Missouri*

chandelier, where he was allowed to go only on Sundays or when there was a party. *(19)*

In 1869, writer and teacher Catherine Beecher, with her sister Harriet Beecher Stowe (who had written *Uncle Tom's Cabin*), published a book of house designs. Called *The American Woman's Home*, these designs were mostly in the Gothic Revival style, but the most interesting feature of the book was that the interiors were designed to make housekeeping easier. Catherine Beecher's houses were "machines for daily life," and she took advantage of several new scientific developments to make them efficient.

Each room was carefully arranged for the use it would have—eating, sleeping, studying, entertaining guests. There were plenty of closets and shelves. Miss Beecher's kitchens were a housewife's dream. They had wall cabinets for storing food and utensils. There were work surfaces where turkeys could be stuffed and pies rolled out. There was a cast-iron cooking stove, an icebox, a sink for washing up. Laundry tubs had their own place in the basement.

These houses had conveniences most people had never enjoyed, or even heard of. Instead of being illuminated by candles or whale oil lamps, they were lit by gas lamps. As for heat, there were still fireplaces in some rooms, but in others there were cast-iron stoves which burned wood or coal. In some of her designs, Miss Beecher also had furnaces in the basement to provide hot air to several rooms at a time. Even more remarkable, there were bathrooms in

19   Theodore Roosevelt Birthplace, New York City

these houses, with toilets and tubs.

Of course, a house like those imagined by Miss Beecher could only be built in the few cities which had gas lines and pipes for bringing in water and sewers for carrying off wastes. And such a house could be built only by a well-to-do family. The average family did not expect to have such comforts and modern conveniences. Poor people living in the crowded slums did not even have all the necessities. Tenements, buildings several stories high with narrow stairways and many small dark rooms, were being constructed in large numbers now for city workers, many of them newcomers to America. Families crowded into these tenements sometimes had to share a single pump on the ground floor for all their water needs. Cooking for the whole family often had to be done over a tiny stove in a corner of the room where everyone ate and slept. In winter the rooms were cold, and in summer they were so hot the tenement dwellers slept on the roof. *(20)*

In the country, life went on much as it always had. If a farmer felt he could spare the money, and his wife had studied the pictures in the ladies' magazines, a new farmhouse might be built for them in something like the Gothic Revival, Italianate, or Second Empire style. But there would be no central heating, gas lights, or indoor toilets. The kitchens would still be country kitchens where food grown on the farm was prepared and cooked over a wood-burning stove and well water was pumped by hand.

Ever-increasing numbers of people moved westward after the Civil War. The government sold land beyond the Missouri River at very low cost, but required the settler to build a permanent home on his property within a short time. There were few trees on the prairies, and hauling in wood was extremely expensive. The Indians who lived on the prairies made earth lodges, covered with sod, and the settlers who came from northern Europe duplicated

20 *Rear tenement in Roosevelt Street, New York City*

the sod houses they remembered from their home countries. From the soil the homesteaders cut out squares of earth held together by strong grass roots. These "bricks" of sod made excellent building material for walls and roofs. Only a small amount of wood was necessary for framing the house. The first "soddie" shelters were crude, but later the homesteaders built fine houses of several rooms. These sod houses withstood the fierce prairie winds and were cool in summer and warm in winter. *(21)*

In later years, when their farms were established and railroads were built into the western territories, the homesteaders had lumber brought in to make wooden houses. The new houses were more pleasing to their owners, but they were really not as suitable to the climate as the houses made of sod bricks, which could withstand the harsh climate for as much as one hundred years.

21   Sod house, Nebraska

7 · THE GILDED AGE

1870–1913

THE MEN WHO AMASSED FORTUNES IN MAN-
ufacturing, mining, lumbering, merchandising, and railroading
were the heroes of the Gilded Age. Not everyone could hope to
become a millionaire, but nearly everyone admired those who were,
especially those who spent their money lavishly. There was as yet
no tax deducted from income to support the expenses of government. Most wealthy people saw no reason why they shouldn't
spend their money on themselves, and they took special pleasure
in spending it on grand houses.

A millionaire was expected to have a great mansion in the city
as well as an estate in the country or at the shore. On New York's
Fifth Avenue, the rich built block-long mansions. On the cliffs
overlooking the ocean in Newport, Rhode Island, they built enormous "cottages" of marble or limestone where they entertained all
summer long with dinner parties and formal balls.

What architect would not be happy to design a house when he
did not have to think about how much it would cost? One of the

51

favorite architects of the very rich was Richard Morris Hunt. He had been trained at the École des Beaux Arts, the School of Fine Arts, in Paris. Here he had learned all about French design and had studied the great palaces, called châteaux, built in France during the Gothic and Renaissance periods. When he came back to America, Hunt could give the Vanderbilts, the Astors, and other wealthy clients just the sort of princely houses they wanted.

William Vanderbilt, whose fortune came from railroads, told Hunt that he and his family were "plain, quiet, unostentatious people" who would be satisfied by something quite simple in the way of architecture. His daughter-in-law, Mrs. Alva Vanderbilt, had other ideas. In 1881, not to be outdone by the rest of New York's society hostesses, she commissioned Hunt to build a French Gothic château for her. It was to become the most extravagantly beautiful house on Fifth Avenue.

Mrs. Vanderbilt's brother-in-law, George, one of the richest men in America, also asked Hunt to design a French château for his 200,000-acre estate in North Carolina. This house, called Biltmore, cost over $4 million. More than one thousand workers and craftsmen, many of them brought over from France, took five years to build it. The house itself covered 5 acres, and was surrounded by superb gardens. Its 250 rooms were filled with paintings, tapestries, and art treasures of all kinds. There was a library for George Vanderbilt's 20,000 books, and a colossal banqueting hall. It was the most magnificent house in the country, though it was not the sort of place where most people would feel at home. (22)

Another well-known architect of this period was Henry Hobson Richardson, who designed many public buildings and railway stations in a style called Neo-Romanesque. This was an eleventh- and twelfth-century European style, earlier than the Gothic, which

22 *Biltmore, Asheville, North Carolina*

imitated old Roman forms to construct very solid buildings. The large private mansions Richardson built were also extremely solid. They were of rough stone or brick, with round arches framing doors and windows. Richardson added towers with pointed roofs, thick columns, and carved stone trim. This kind of house soon could be found in every city or town where a well-to-do family wished to be housed in dignified fashion. *(23)*

Richardson's Romanesque style was also frequently used for row houses. But the architect designed a few houses which were quite different: They were smaller and simpler, and their exteriors were covered with wooden shingles which were allowed to weather naturally to a soft silver-gray color. The shingled house was later to prove very popular.

One of the younger architects who followed Richardson was the energetic and imaginative Stanford White. With his partners Charles McKim and William Mead, White designed scores of great buildings (among them Grand Central Station in New

53

York), as well as sumptuous houses. White and his partners were masters at borrowing ideas from Renaissance architecture and creating houses that were strikingly handsome and richly ornamented. They had sculptors and artists working with them in making carvings and statues that were integral parts of the house design. Their clients were delighted with the elegant results, which they felt reflected the expansive spirit of the times in America.

New York and Newport were not the only places where luxurious architecture flourished. In Chicago, there were millionaires too, but they were not so interested in spending their money on splendid houses. They *were* interested in commissioning impressive buildings for their businesses, offices, and department stores. With

the development of steel as a building material, and elevators that could reach new heights, it was possible to build "cloud scrapers" as much as twenty stories high. By and large, inventive Chicago architects and engineers turned their energies to working out the problems of constructing such buildings rather than designing houses. But their success in commercial building helped make possible a new kind of housing, the many-storied apartment house. People who did not want to take care of a house and grounds, or could not afford to do so, could live in several rooms in an apartment house. Many city dwellers throughout the nation found this a very convenient way of living.

As land opened up in the Southwest, vast ranches were established with herds of cattle ranging over thousands of acres. The ranch owner's house was sometimes in a style derived from old Spanish country houses. A long low building was built of adobe, with a porch all along the front to provide shade from the blazing sun. Cowboys slept in a bunkhouse near the main ranch house when they were not riding the trails. *(24)*

23   *(left) Neo-Romanesque house, Chicago, Illinois*   24   *(below) Ranch house, Fredericksburg, Texas*

Farther west in California, a few of the old Spanish churches built by missionaries in the seventeenth and eighteenth centuries were still to be found. These simple buildings of white-plastered adobe with thick walls giving shelter from the heat were well suited to the climate of southern California. As this part of the country became more settled, new houses were built in something of the same style, using cement and stucco instead of adobe. They had tile roofs, arched windows and doorways, enclosed patios, and iron grillwork. This was known as Spanish colonial or Mission architecture. *(25)*

The lively city of San Francisco was full of people who had made money in railroads, real estate, and gold mining. Up and down the hilly streets they built all kinds of houses—Italianate, Second Empire, Gothic Revival, and Queen Anne. The Queen Anne style, popular all over the country, was supposedly based on the architecture of the reign of an eighteenth-century queen of England. Actually, it was a mixture of many styles. A Queen Anne house was tall, with gabled roofs, heavy chimneys, and frequently a round tower or two. Different materials were used, with the first floor built perhaps of stone or bricks, the upper stories of wood, shingle, or stucco. A porch was wrapped around the first floor, and sometimes there were panes of stained glass in the windows. *(26)*

North of San Francisco, lumberman William Carson made his fortune cutting down giant redwood trees. Redwood is a fine building material, very durable, resistant to termites and fire. When Carson built his eighteen-room mansion in Eureka, California in 1886, of course it was of redwood. He probably designed it himself, and it certainly can be called fanciful. There are bits of numerous styles, including Gothic Revival and Queen Anne. There are all kinds of towers, peaked gables, bulging pillars,

25 (top) "Spanish Colonial" house, San Francisco, California   26 (bottom) Isaac Bell House, McKim, Mead & White, Architects, Newport, Rhode Island

balconies, railings, and porches, with quantities of scrollwork trim. It was described in newspapers of the day as the finest house in the West. *(27)*

As the country grew in the last years of the nineteenth century and the first of the twentieth, there was a tremendous boom in building. Up to then, most houses had been built individually. The owner, sometimes with an architect, decided on the design, and the carpenter-builder made the parts of the house and put

27   (above) Carson House, Eureka, California   28   (right) Bungalow, California

them together. Now it was possible to look at a catalogue and order parts from a factory where machines turned out great quantities of housing materials in standard sizes. The lumber might come from the West, the roofing from Chicago, the windows and doors from Connecticut. This meant that in many different locations there would be hundreds of houses with parts exactly alike though they were put together differently. And it meant that there was no longer such a demand for craftsmen who could make the parts carefully piece by piece. Because factory-made parts were cheaper, such houses generally did not cost so much. This was important, for as the population increased rapidly and people were paid better wages, there was a great need for thousands of inexpensive new homes.

Property prices in the city rose higher as land became scarcer, so people moved farther out into the country. Trains and trolleys could take them back and forth to work from the new communities that were called suburbs. People still had houses built individually, but now a contractor-builder might build one house or a dozen or more and then advertise for buyers.

The houses that sprang up everywhere in the suburbs were of every imaginable kind. You could live in a home with all the modern conveniences, one that looked on the outside like a Cape Codder or a saltbox, a Georgian, Federal, or Greek Revival house, a Dutch or Spanish colonial house, or any other style that happened to please you. Some houses, particularly on the West Coast, were built in Chinese or Japanese styles. Suburban homes usually had neat front lawns and a backyard where family activities took place.

Another type that began to be seen everywhere in suburbs and towns was the bungalow. This was a small one-story house with a heavy gable over the entrance. There was often a front porch with its own gable. The word bungalow comes from India where it meant a traveler's rest house. There were many Americans who were glad to take their rest in this kind of snug little house. *(28)*

8 · FRANK LLOYD WRIGHT

1869–1959

FRANK LLOYD WRIGHT IS OFTEN CALLED America's greatest architect. He was born in Wisconsin and went to work in Chicago as an architect in 1891. Wright was an arrogant genius who declared, "You've got to have guts to be an architect. People will come to you and tell you what they want, and you will have to give them what they need."

What they needed, in Wright's opinion, was a totally different kind of architecture from what they were used to. No more Greek columns, imitation castles, mansard roofs, cupolas, or gingerbread trim. A house should be organic, Wright said. It should look as if it grew right out of the site where it was built, and all its parts should contribute to a harmonious whole.

Frank Lloyd Wright spent his boyhood summers on his grandfather's farm. He loved the land and the wide horizons of the prairie. He wanted the houses he designed to be rooted in the land yet allow the people who lived in them to have space to move around freely. Instead of arranging rooms in a cube around a center hallway, Wright stretched his rooms out in several directions, experimenting with different kinds of floor plans. He saw that with modern central heating there was no need for rooms to be closed up for warmth, and plate glass was making large window spaces possible.

Wright insisted on "breaking the box" of traditional house and room shapes. And he acted on the teaching of Louis Sullivan, a Chicago architect with whom he worked as a young man. Sullivan had said that "form follows function," that is, architectural forms should be shaped by the uses to which they would be put, not covered up or disguised to look like something else.

The shape of many of Wright's houses was long and low, with strong horizontal lines. Sometimes the roofs extended out almost like wings, yet the houses always looked very solid and protective. Wright used natural materials such as stone and wood inside and out, without paint or meaningless decoration.

Inside, low ceilings often exposed massive beams in bold patterns. There was much open space, and few interior walls. Large fireplaces were constructed of rough brick or stone. Deep-set windows were placed in such a way as to allow a play of light and shadow within the rooms. Skylights and clerestories (windows placed high up in the wall) let in sunlight in interesting formations. There were built-in benches, tables, and bookcases. The warm colors of natural wood and the textures of stone, cement, and brick were simple and dramatic.

At first, people were shocked by Wright's ideas. But gradually a few brave ones asked him to design their houses. People began to discover that Wright's houses were well suited to the more informal kind of lives they were now beginning to live.

Wright was asked to design many important buildings in addition to houses. His ideas influenced other architects here and abroad. They no longer felt they had to design houses based on some style of the past. Because Wright had been bold, they too could be more open about expressing new ideas. The two houses Wright built for himself, Taliesin East in Wisconsin and Taliesin West in Arizona, were visited by many architects, and Wright trained others in his studios there. The architect lived a long and active life and was still designing in his eighties.

All of Wright's houses are original and interesting, but perhaps the most fascinating and most famous is a house he built in Pennsylvania for a department store executive in 1936. It is called Falling Water, for it is set beside a tumbling mountain stream. The house is built mostly of rough stone, with white concrete slabs projecting out over the water. There is a sense of great power in the way Wright has arranged the forms, yet its natural materials make it seem a part of the woodland setting. *(29)*

Frank Lloyd Wright had a vision of changing American architecture so that it would be true to the values he thought most important. He believed in buildings designed to meet the real human needs for shelter, space, comfort, beauty, orderly simplicity, honest materials, no distracting frills, intelligent and imaginative living arrangements, and unity of the whole. Other architects had some of the same concepts, but more than anyone else Wright was responsible for an entirely new direction in the way America builds its houses.

29 *Frank Lloyd Wright house, "Falling Water," Bear Run, Pennsylvania*

9 · A NEW LOOK

1913–1940

IN ADDITION TO THE INFLUENCE OF FRANK
Lloyd Wright, other factors were changing the architecture of
America in the twentieth century. The Gilded Age came to an
end in 1913, shortly before the outbreak of World War I. It was
much harder to make a fortune now that so much of the country's
iron and coal, timberlands, oil fields, and railways had already
been developed. And in 1920 Congress passed a law requiring
the payment of income tax, so it was no longer possible to keep
all one's money to oneself.

There were fewer and fewer châteaux built now, for the old
mansions were proving very costly to keep up, and it was increasingly difficult to find anyone willing to work as a servant. A number
of the enormous houses of the Gilded Age were turned into schools,
museums, convents, apartments, and clubhouses. Others were torn
down to make way for urban skyscrapers or housing tracts in the
country. As highways were constructed and more people had au-
tomobiles, the old suburbs grew larger and new ones were estab-

lished. The houses in these suburbs were mostly imitations of traditional American or English styles, the most popular being the Georgian "colonial" house.

But some architects were trying completely new ways of designing. In Europe a group called the International School was experimenting with buildings constructed of steel, reinforced concrete, and glass. One of their leaders was Walter Gropius, who taught at the German Bauhaus, or architectural institute. The houses these designers built were blocks with smooth white surfaces. The very large windows were an integral part of the walls, not just holes in them. There was no decoration to distract the eye. The designers wanted the beauty of the building to be in its pure basic form and not "added on." They believed in the statement of one of their number, Mies van der Rohe, who proclaimed that "less is more."

In the 1920s and 30s, Gropius and several members of the International School came to the United States to live. They designed buildings in what came to be called the Bauhaus style. Some people thought it boxy and cold. Others liked the clean simple look and the way the glass walls seemed to bring the outdoors inside, permitting the dweller to feel close to nature.

In California, one of the European architects, Richard Neutra, designed a house for Dr. Philip Lovell in 1928. Dr. Lovell was a well-known writer of books on health, and he wanted his house to be filled with fresh air and sunshine. Built on a steep hillside overlooking the Pacific Ocean, the house is cement over a steel frame. It is large, but light and airy looking. Dr. Lovell called it Health House, and after it was built other houses with glass walls in the International style began to appear all around the country. *(30)*

The Bauhaus designs were not popular with everyone. Most

people were not enthusiastic about a "machine for living in," preferring the kinds of architecture with which they were familiar. But when the Depression came in the thirties, millions lost their jobs and fewer houses of any kind were built then or later, during World War II.

30 *Lovell Health House, Richard Neutra, Architect, Los Angeles, California*

10 · MORE AND MORE: THE BUILDING BOOM

1945–1970

AFTER WORLD WAR II THERE WAS ANOTHER period of great prosperity. Wages were higher than they had ever been before. White workers moved from tenements to the suburbs in great numbers, and southern black workers went north to find jobs in the cities. Developers bought up cornfields and pastures, bulldozed them, and put up thousands of houses as close to each other as possible and as fast as they could be nailed together. The lots were small and so were the houses, but the new owners were glad to have their own private property.

In the new developments could be found a number of house styles. One was the Cape Codder, which might look something like the old-fashioned New England house but which did not have the big central chimney and fireplaces that were the heart of the colonial home. Another was a single-story house with low roofline which might have a paved space in back called a patio. This was known as the ranch house, though it was far from the plains of Texas. Still another kind was the split-level, one story high in one section and two stories in the rest; it had no attic, cellar, or porch.

The ranch house and the split-level did not stick to the old-fashioned arrangement of rooms. Instead of closed-off parlor, dining room, and kitchen, there were family living spaces that opened into each other. There might be no walls at all between living room, dining area, and kitchen. Quite a few of these houses had large "picture windows" in the living room.

All these new houses were heated by oil, gas, or electricity, and many had air conditioning. Kitchens were equipped with gas or electric stoves, refrigerators, dishwashers, and machines for laundering. There was a garage or parking space for each house, for most suburban workers had to drive to their jobs.

Millions of people were now far more comfortably housed than they had ever been. But because the houses were put up all at once by developers interested only in making money, these new housing complexes did not give communities the character of towns which had grown naturally. There was not the close neighborly feeling of a village where people lived in the same place they worked and where everybody knew each other. *(31)*

Meanwhile, the cities were in trouble. With so many people moving out, buildings began to be neglected. Landlords and developers did not want to spend money on city housing, so government money was made available to help pay for fixing up old buildings and constructing new ones. A few of the new low-rent apartment buildings were well designed, even though the architects had to try to save as much as possible in building costs. But many of the designers did not think enough about the needs of the people who would live in these apartments. There was not enough space, light, privacy, security, or beauty to make people content to live there.

In both city and country there was a new interest in saving old buildings. For a long time whenever a house grew old or just

31   Levittown, Long Island, New York

became out of date, it was either torn down or left empty to decay. Now building costs were rising tremendously. Lumber, bricks, cement, steel, glass, insulation, plumbing fixtures—all cost more each year. Carpenters, plumbers, and masons were now paid as much in an hour as they used to get for a full day's work. So people began to look for old houses that were not too badly deteriorated in order to restore them to usefulness at less than it would cost to build a new one. As they looked around, they discovered many fine old places worth saving, and they began to have an appreciation of the architectural styles and the workmanship of homes of the past.

With building—and land—costs increasing so alarmingly, one solution was the mobile home. This was a factory-made house that could be hitched to a truck and taken anywhere the owner wanted to put it. If the owner had to move, he could take his house with him. A mobile home had to be long and narrow so that it could travel along highways. It had a metal frame and a metal exterior covering. There were two or three rooms which opened into each other like a railway car. Early mobile homes had flat roofs and no trimming, but later they were designed to look more like standard houses, with clapboards of metal, gables, and even shutters at the windows. Many mobile homes today are never moved except from the factory to the sites where they are set on foundations. Mobile homes do not last as long as permanent houses.

Another kind of less expensive home is the prefabricated house. All its parts, except for wiring and plumbing, are made in a factory and then shipped to its destination, where it is then set up on a foundation and assembled by the owner or a local builder. The new owner can choose a prefabricated house from a number of simple architectural styles, and save a good deal of money by doing the carpentry and painting himself.

32　Condominium, Hardy Holzman Pfeiffer Associates, Architects, Cincinnati, Ohio

Still another type of housing that became popular in the 1970s was the condominium. Sometimes a condominium is a building in which apartments are bought instead of rented. Sometimes it is a group of houses built in a row like the city houses of the nineteenth century. Usually of wood, they may be in "modern" style or imitations of Georgian row houses. Using a smaller amount of land than a single-family dwelling, the condominium cuts costs by sharing walls and sometimes heating systems. The condominium owner does not have to worry about upkeep or lawn mowing, since that is taken care of by a manager whose salary is paid by all the residents. *(32)*

11 · A PLACE IN THE SUN

ALTHOUGH $4-MILLION CHÂTEAUX WERE obsolete by the 1960s, there were more houses with more expensive conveniences and gadgets being built all the time. Some people began to question whether this was a good thing. They were worried about the environment. Too many houses were being built on good farmland, on hillsides where they caused erosion, or in the dry Southwest where they were using up too much water. And too many natural resources such as lumber and ore were being also used up. The factories that produced materials and fittings for these houses required a lot of power to operate, and after the houses were built, the owners used large amounts of electricity, oil, natural gas, and water to keep them running. Although there had always been enough of everything in the United States up to now, we might some day run out.

In the 1970s, the cost of fuel oil went so high that many home owners with oil-burning furnaces had to spend more money than they could afford, just to keep warm. Natural gas and electricity also became very expensive. It was clear that this country needed a cheaper way of keeping houses heated.

72

"Why not use the sun?" suggested the engineers who had been experimenting with solar heat. "It's free."

Sunlight is free, but it has to be collected, stored, and then distributed if it is to be put to use. Several different ways of doing this have been worked out. First, the house must face south to get the maximum amount of sunlight. The most common way to trap the sunlight is by putting heat-collecting panels of glass or metal on a south-facing roof. Sunlight then will strike the panels to warm water or liquid which is piped into the house to be used right away or to be stored in a tank. Because the sun does not shine every day, a solar-heated house usually has to have a small furnace or stove to help out when needed. But the sun can provide at least half the heat and hot water used in the house. A solar system may cost a good deal to install, but it costs practically nothing to run. *(33)*

Even without solar heat collectors, the sun can do a great deal to warm a house if there are windows of double glass facing south. Every house can also save heat by having plenty of good insulating material between inner and outer walls to help hold the heat inside.

When architects design houses today, they are thinking not only about style, but also of how well they can conserve energy.

33   Solar house, Massachusetts

12 · TODAY AND TOMORROW

IN 1973 A BOOK WAS PUBLISHED CALLED
Small Is Beautiful. The author, E. F. Schumacher, was not just
talking about size. He meant that we should not have such big
ideas about what we need. We can, he said, live more simply,
get along with less. We can stop selfishly using up so many of the
earth's resources. We can start thinking about people in the rest
of the world, and about what will be left for everybody's children
and grandchildren.

A lot of thoughtful people agree that small is beautiful. When
it comes to building a house, they want something simple that will
fit into the environment. It must not use a lot of energy, and it must
not cost a lot of money. For them, the best way may be to build
their own house.

All over the country today, people are designing houses for
themselves that will be just as big as they need but no bigger.
They teach themselves how to be carpenters and masons. They
may use lumber from an old barn, or windows and doors from old

34   *Handhewn house, Woodstock, New York*

houses. The kitchen is simple, probably with a woodburning cook-stove. Sometimes they do without running water, using a pump instead. Some people use kerosene lamps or candles instead of electric lights. Others use electricity generated by windmills on their property.

These people are returning to old ways of living in homes something like those of our early settlers. Some owner-built homes are like log cabins the pioneers built; some are built partially underground to conserve heat; others are in a triangular shape called an A-frame. But usually they are of no particular style. They look like what they are—simple, handmade, and honest. And that can be beautiful. *(34)*

As we look back at the history of American architecture, we see that it changed as the country changed. People's needs at first were very basic—simple shelter in a world new to them. But with the passage of time, America became more settled and prosperous and people wanted more than shelter. They wanted space, convenience, beauty, and style. They wanted to feel a connection with the great art and architecture of the past, and at the same time they wanted to express their pride in American independence.

A high point was reached in the nineteenth century with houses becoming larger and more elaborate than at any time before or since. In the twentieth century, new technologies made American houses increasingly comfortable, with improved heating and well-equipped bathrooms and kitchens. But today the dwindling of natural resources is again having an impact on our way of living.

We still depend a great deal on technology today, but we are going back to doing more for ourselves. We are beginning to have some understanding of our real needs. Our lives will have to be made simpler, and our architecture will be simplified too.

We understand that houses built now cannot be copies of the styles of the past. When we find a Georgian house, a Greek or Gothic Revival house, a Frank Lloyd Wright house, we can enjoy its beauty and its special character. But our needs are different from those of the people who built them, our times are not theirs. We will use our inventiveness to solve our housing problems. The possibilities are exciting and the results will not be merely imitations of what has gone before.

We will create our own style for the America of today.

INDEX

NOTE: Page numbers in italics refer to illus-
trations.